INTRODUCTION

"You could write the entire story of civil rights by going back to the history of the city of St. Louis."
—Judge Nathan B. Young, *The St. Louis American*, 1964

Imagine slaves who stood up to their owners for their freedom. Picture women and men who sat inside restaurants that refused to serve black people, day after day, to make a point. Think of workers protesting outside of businesses that wouldn't hire people with the "wrong" skin color. Imagine students fighting for the right to go to the college of their choice.

All of these things really happened in St. Louis. They're part of what makes the struggle for civil rights in our city so powerful. Ordinary men and women saw how people were being treated unfairly. Instead of sitting by, they took extraordinary action to create positive change so everyone could have equal civil rights.

So what are civil rights? They're the rights we all have as Americans to ensure we're treated fairly. They're also real things you run into every day, like the freedom to:

- go to school
- ride a bus
- go to a movie theater
- rent an apartment or buy a house
- get a job
- eat out at a restaurant
- vote for government leaders

But people haven't always had *equal* civil rights in the United States. African Americans have long been given either different or separate rights—if any at all. But they've always pushed back, both on their own and with help from people of many backgrounds. This is especially true in St. Louis.

Local people and events that happened here changed the daily lives of all Americans. These changes started even before Missouri was a state! And they're still happening today.

This book will introduce you to St. Louis's often-overlooked civil rights history. You'll meet brave men and women who spoke out and fought back. You may already know some of their names. Take a good look at your school, post office, or a park or playground you like. There's a good chance that place was named after a local civil rights activist, like Marian Oldham, Norman Seay, or James Milton Turner.

These activists worked hard to change things. They *advocated* for their rights, which means they spoke up when they saw something wrong. They demanded fair treatment and tried many different ways to get it. The problems they faced, and the actions they took, shaped this city. In some cases they even shaped this country!

Of course, we can't cover every piece of St. Louis's civil rights history in these pages. That would make for one really long book. We help you figure out where to go from here in the last chapter.

A couple of final notes:

- The words used to refer to African Americans have changed over time, from "colored" to "Negro" to "black" to "African American." Whenever we include a story or letter from a certain time period, you'll see the word people used at that time.

- You'll also see the words "slave" and "enslaved" throughout the book. "Slave" was used more often in the past. Today, more people use "enslaved." This shift shows how being enslaved was just one part of who these individuals were—their whole identities were about more than just being "slaves."

We hope you'll be inspired by the stories you're about to read. We know we were.

—Amanda and Melanie

 What are some civil rights you have that are worth fighting for?

CHAPTER 1
SLAVERY AND "FREEDOM" IN THE 1800S

The earliest fights for civil rights in our country were all about slavery. Black people were brought here from the continent of Africa and forced to work for free for their white owners as slaves. They were thought of as property. They weren't looked at as human—at least not in the same way white people were.

Slaves had little control over their lives. Their owners decided many things for them, from what they could do to when they could do it. Slaves also lived in places that were dirty, harsh, and unsafe. Worse yet, enslaved families could be ripped apart at any time. Moms, dads, or children could be sold to different owners or sent somewhere else to work and live.

Rarely, enslaved people could become free. Some were freed in their owners' wills after the owners died. Others bought their freedom, but this was very hard to do because it cost so much. (Case in point: The price of an enslaved woman in 1850 was $1,000—today that would be over $30,000!) Enslaved blacks could also run away to *free states*, places where slavery was illegal.

A small group of free African Americans came to St. Louis because it was a major city close to the free state of Illinois. Some of them became

STANDING UP FOR
CIVIL RIGHTS
IN ST. LOUIS

Amanda E. Doyle and
Melanie A. Adams

To Anna & Noelle — Always stand up for what is right!

Missouri History Museum Press
St. Louis
Distributed by University of Chicago Press

Amanda E. Doyle

TABLE OF CONTENTS

Introduction   3

Chapter 1: Slavery and "Freedom" in the 1800s   6

Chapter 2: Missouri's Battle for Statehood—and Slavery   8

Chapter 3: Suing for Freedom   12

Chapter 4: Missouri in the Civil War   19

Chapter 5: Life after the Civil War   22

Chapter 6: Moving Through and To St. Louis   26

Chapter 7: Fighting for Equal Schools   30

Chapter 8: Fighting for Equal Housing   42

Chapter 9: Fighting for Equal Work   55

Chapter 10: Fighting for Equal Entertainment   64

Chapter 11: What's Next?   70

Chapter 12: What Can You Do?   73

Recommended Reading   74

Index   75

rich and influential, but even they weren't seen as equal to whites.

Free blacks in St. Louis had to have a license to live here. They could only live in certain places and be outside at certain times. They couldn't vote in elections or speak out against whites in court cases. Free black children couldn't even go to school or learn how to read. All of these rules likely left some free African Americans wondering how "free" they really were.

Elizabeth "Lizzie" Keckley bought her and her son's freedom for $1,200. She later became the trusted dressmaker and friend of First Lady Mary Todd Lincoln. Missouri Historical Society.

How would you define freedom so that "free" people all have the same civil rights?

7

CHAPTER 2
MISSOURI'S BATTLE FOR STATEHOOD—AND SLAVERY

The United States started in 1776 with just 13 states along the Atlantic Ocean. People who wanted more land on which to build, farm, and hunt moved west. These new places where settlers had moved were called *territories*.

Over time the territories asked to join the United States. Slavery was legal in some of the new states but illegal in others.

By 1818, when the Missouri Territory had enough people in it to ask to become a state, many U.S. leaders wanted to end slavery (even those who had slaves). Some wanted to set slaves free very soon.

This was a problem for many of the people in the Missouri Territory who had come from the south. They were used to slavery being legal and assumed it would be allowed in their new state. They made money off of slave labor and feared ending slavery would change how they lived. But anti-slavery groups didn't want to keep adding slave states to the country at a time when they thought slavery should be over.

People on both sides of the issue argued strongly for their views throughout 1819. In St. Louis, a group of anti-slavery blacks and whites protested on the steps of the Old Courthouse. This was the first civil rights protest in the country!

Map of the United States and its territories from 1818. Library of Congress Geography and Map Division.

In Washington, DC, members of Congress had different ideas for how Missouri could become a state. One plan had two parts: stop new slaves from coming to Missouri and free the enslaved people already there at age 25. Missouri's leaders didn't like this option. Unable to agree, Congress took a break, leaving Missouri's request for statehood unanswered.

The 1819 anti-slavery protest at the Old Courthouse.

By the time Congress went back to work in late 1819, Maine had asked to become a state too. Now Congress could make a deal for both new states. This deal is called the Missouri Compromise. It said that as of March 1820:

- Maine was a new free state.
- Missouri was a new slave state.
- All the western territories north of Missouri's southern border were free territories.

Many people thought ending slavery would make America stronger. What's a civil right we have today that makes our country strong?

VIEWS & NEWS

What did people say at the time about slavery and the Missouri Compromise?

A pro-slavery view from South Carolina senator Charles Pinckney: "[Slavery] cannot be got rid of without ruining the country. . . . The great body of slaves are happier in their present situation than they could be in any other, and the man or men who would attempt to give them freedom, would be their greatest enemies."

An anti-slavery take from New York representative James Tallmadge: "Extend *slavery*, this bane of man, over your extended empire, and you turn its accumulated strength into positive weakness; you put poison in your bosom; you place a vulture on your heart. . . ."

Here's what President James Monroe wrote to former president Thomas Jefferson about the issue on February 19, 1820: "I have never known a question so menacing to the tranquility and even the continuance of our Union." Jefferson responded that "like a fire bell in the night, [the Missouri Question] awakened and filled me with terror. I considered it at once as the [death] knell of the Union."

CHAPTER 3
SUING FOR FREEDOM

Because Missouri was a slave state, slavery remained a part of St. Louis life in the mid-1800s. Slave auctions happened on the Old Courthouse steps, and slave-catchers searched for runaway slaves so they could return them for a reward. Laws were also passed to control what enslaved people could do. One law said they couldn't be taught to read or write. Another said they couldn't be legally married. (This meant that husbands and wives could be sold separately.) Black people also couldn't meet to worship without a white person present.

The Last Sale of Slaves by Thomas S. Noble, ca. 1880. Missouri Historical Society.

ELIJAH P. LOVEJOY (1802–1837)

Elijah P. Lovejoy was a white minister who believed slavery was evil. He often wrote against slavery in his newspaper, the *St. Louis Observer*. In response, pro-slavery whites threatened him and tried to destroy his printing press several times in 1836.

Lovejoy moved his newspaper across the Mississippi River to Alton, Illinois. The threats and violence followed. In 1837 a white mob attacked his new newspaper office and killed him. The attackers also threw the printing press into the river.

You can find a monument to Lovejoy in Alton today. Plaques nearby tell

HERE AND NOW

his story, and a unique "whispering bench" lets people sitting on opposite sides of the monument hear each other speaking clearly.

Enslaved people fought back. Some tried to fight or hurt their owners. Others ran away. Some protested in public. Others filed *freedom suits*. These were lawsuits against slave owners in the hopes of winning legal freedom. Freedom suits were some of the first civil rights court cases in the country.

Both men and women filed freedom suits. Enslaved mothers were especially eager to be freed so they could pass on their free status to their children.

Many freedom suits happened in St. Louis because it was a big place with courts and lawyers. Enslaved blacks passing through the busy river city could learn from free blacks living there how to use the court system to earn their freedom. Slaves running errands in town for their owners could also slip into a lawyer's office to ask questions or get advice.

Enslaved people often argued that they should be free because they had once lived in free territories or states. That's exactly what happened in the first freedom suit to reach the Missouri Supreme Court. It was filed by a woman named Winny in 1821. Winny said she had been taken as a slave from Kentucky to the Northwest Territory (now Illinois) for four years. Her owners then moved her to St. Louis. Winny asked to be freed because she had lived in free land for so long. The court agreed and freed her in 1824.

Thanks to Winny, the idea of "once free, always free" became common. Courts followed it until the famous case of Dred and Harriet Scott.

✎ *By the mid-1800s, black people in St. Louis were denied the right to read and write. How do you think this affected the lives of enslaved people?*

ST. LOUIS, CIVIL RIGHTS, AND THE U.S. SUPREME COURT:
SCOTT V. SANDFORD

Portrait of Dred Scott by Louis Schultze, ca. 1890. Missouri Historical Society.

THE PEOPLE

- Dred and Harriet Scott, married slaves
- Irene Emerson, the widow of the Scotts' former owner
- John Sanford, Emerson's brother (whose last name was misspelled by the court clerk)

THE BACKGROUND

Dred and Harriet Scott belonged to many families over the years, including the Emersons. At one point, they had lived in free states (Illinois and Minnesota, where they got married) due to their owner's work travels. Because of this, the Scotts wanted to claim their freedom. They were counting on the "once free, always free" idea to win their case.

They filed a freedom suit in Missouri in 1846. They fought in the courts for years, until Missouri's federal court of appeals upheld a ruling that said the Scotts weren't free. They had one last hope: the U.S. Supreme Court.

THE CASE

In 1854, Dred Scott and his lawyers filed a lawsuit in the Supreme Court. They wanted the Court to give the final answer to two questions:

- Did time living in a free state make a person free forever?
- Could Negroes of African descent be called U.S. citizens? (If not, they would have no legal right to file lawsuits in the first place.)

Sanford's lawyers said both questions were pointless. They argued that Congress couldn't control slavery because the U.S. Constitution regarded slaves as property. This meant slaves' rights were the states' concern, not the Court's.

THE DECISION

On March 6, 1857, the Court decided that the Constitution's authors didn't intend for blacks to be citizens. This meant blacks didn't have the rights of citizens. Because Dred Scott was black, he wasn't a citizen and couldn't file a lawsuit in the U.S. legal system.

THE AFTERMATH

Emerson sold the Scotts to Taylor Blow, the son of their former owner. He set them and their children free right away. Dred Scott died as a free man shortly afterward. Harriet lived until 1876.

THE LEGACY

Pro-slavery people and anti-slavery people had a hard time agreeing before *Scott v. Sandford*. After the ruling, they got even angrier with each other.

Anti-slavery people were upset that states got to decide important things like rights and equality. They wanted the federal government to do that. But pro-slavery people believed strongly in the government staying out of states' business.

At the state level, the *Scott* case was argued inside the Old Courthouse in downtown St. Louis. A life-size bronze statue of Dred and Harriet Scott now stands outside the courthouse. It's the first—and only—statue of the couple anywhere in the world.

CHAPTER 4

MISSOURI IN THE CIVIL WAR

The fight over slavery was at the heart of the Civil War. The 11 Southern states that didn't want to give up their slaves split apart from the country. They formed their own government, led by Jefferson Davis, and called themselves the Confederate states.

The 23 Northern states, called the Union states, stayed with the U.S. government under President Abraham Lincoln. Of these, 19 were free states, but the other 4 were slave states. These states—Delaware, Kentucky, Maryland, and Missouri—were referred to as *border states*, because they were right where the Northern border met the Southern border.

The North and the South each wanted to keep the border states on "their" side. This made border states sites of fierce battles and uncertainty. One day you could be accused of being a traitor to the North. The next day your home could be raided by Southern troops looking for supplies and weapons. Also, friends, neighbors, and even families were often ripped apart by fights about what should happen in the country.

What do you think daily life was like for St. Louisans whose neighbors, friends, or family were on opposite sides of the Civil War?

VIEWS & NEWS

Men from Missouri fought on both sides of the war. Black men fought too. Some were in the Southern army, perhaps because their owners made them. But most were in the Northern army.

An enslaved man named Samuel Cobble left his owner in Brunswick, Missouri, to fight for the North in the Massachusetts 55th Infantry. In a letter home to his enslaved wife, he shared his hopes for a future free of slavery:

"... though great is the present national difficulties yet I look foward to a brighter day When i shall have the opertunity of seeing you in the full enjoyment of freedom I would like to no if you are still in slavery if you are it will not be long before we shall have crushed the system that now opreses you for in the course of three months you shall have your liberty. great is the outpouring of the colored people that is now rallying with the hearts of lions against that very curse that has separated you an me yet we shall meet again and oh what a happy time that will be when this unGodly rebellion shall be put down and the curses of our land is trampled under our feet i am a soldier now and i shall use my utmost endeavers to strike at the rebellion and the heart of this system that so long has kept us in chains. ..."

In July 1861, President Lincoln put Major General John C. Frémont in charge of Missouri. The next month Frémont declared *martial law*. This meant the military made the state's rules, not Missouri's leaders. Under Frémont, all property owned by traitors was to be taken. If enslaved people were part of that property, they were to be freed instantly. This made Frémont's order the country's first Emancipation Proclamation. But President Lincoln wanted to move more slowly, so he forced Frémont to take back the order in September and then put someone else in charge of Missouri.

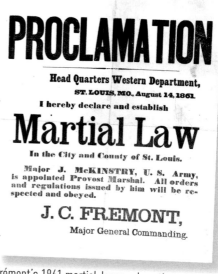

Frémont's 1861 martial-law proclamation. Missouri Historical Society.

Over a year later, President Lincoln made his famous Emancipation Proclamation. On paper it freed all slaves living in the South. But because the Southern states wouldn't listen to the U.S. president, it didn't really free anyone there. It didn't free slaves in Missouri either, because Missouri was in the North, and it applied only to the South.

As the Civil War came to an end, Missouri's leaders knew change was coming. They wanted to help define their own future. At a January 1865 meeting to update the state's laws and rules, they approved a law that ended slavery in the state. This means Missouri banned slavery almost a whole year before the 13th Amendment to the U.S. Constitution ended slavery nationwide.

CHAPTER 5
LIFE AFTER THE CIVIL WAR

The Civil War ended in May 1865. The North had won. The defeated Southern states now had to follow many rules set by the North. This was the start of a period known as *Reconstruction*. (Missouri and the other border states didn't have to follow these rules because they had stayed in the United States.)

In 1868 the 14th Amendment was added to the U.S. Constitution. It made citizens of "all persons born or naturalized in the United States." Finally there was an answer to the question of whether black Americans were citizens! Yet they still couldn't vote in elections, even in Missouri. This changed in 1870, when the 15th Amendment to the U.S. Constitution gave men of every race the right to vote.

Neither amendment changed how blacks and whites interacted though. Many white people all over the country still treated African Americans as *inferior*. This means they acted like blacks were on a lower level than them.

In both the North and the South, many laws were passed to keep different races away from each other. This separation, called *segregation*, was everywhere, from restaurants and theaters to train cars and bathrooms.

St. Louis didn't have many of these laws. It kept blacks and whites apart out of custom. That's "just the way it was." Restaurants, hotels, factories, and theaters might—or might not—be open to all. Or they might be open to all only sometimes. Habits and a few laws also kept blacks and whites separate at school, in neighborhoods, at work, and at play.

All of this explains why St. Louis was often called "a Northern city in a Southern state." It accepted African Americans as citizens, but it didn't treat them as equals.

The city's streetcars are a perfect example. White riders could sit inside, but black riders had to hang on to the outside. This was dangerous because the streetcars were pulled by horses. If you fell off the side of a streetcar, there was a good chance you'd get trampled by a horse!

Some black streetcar riders fought back in the courts. One man, Charlton Tandy, tried something different. He started standing near streetcar stops where African Americans were waiting. If it looked like a streetcar driver was going to pass by without stopping, Tandy would reach out and grab the horse's reins to force the driver to stop.

He also got groups of black people to *boycott*, or stop using streetcars and go places on foot instead. He wanted to get the streetcar owners' attention and force change by taking fare money away from them. The owners' responded by changing their policies—slowly.

Does segregation still exist? Where or when do you see blacks and whites living separately? What do we lose when we live separate lives?

CHARLTON TANDY (1836–1919)

Charlton Tandy was an early civil rights leader in St. Louis. He did many things:

- He led slaves to freedom on the Underground Railroad.
- He served in the military in Missouri during the Civil War.
- He co-founded Lincoln Institute (now Lincoln University) to help train black teachers.
- He organized the Colored Refugee Relief Board to aid African Americans fleeing the South.
- He helped *integrate*, or bring together, blacks and whites in St. Louis's public schools and post offices.

The *St. Louis Post-Dispatch* even ran a story on him when he died. This was surprising because the white-owned paper didn't cover news about black people.

You may have seen Tandy's name around town. Tandy Park, in the Ville neighborhood, is named for him. Over at the Saint Louis Zoo, you can ride the Tandy engine. It's Zooline Railroad Engine No. 49.

CHAPTER 6
MOVING THROUGH AND TO ST. LOUIS

Life in the South was very hard for African Americans. They were free, but they didn't have equal rights. Jobs were tough to find. People didn't have enough money to live on. Some blacks even felt threatened by white Southerners who tried to control or hurt them.

By 1879 thousands of black men, women, and children wanted to escape the South. Their search for safety and equality took them north. More and more African American migrants arrived on the banks of the Mississippi River at St. Louis. Many were on their way to Kansas. Most had no money and no contacts to help them.

Charlton Tandy, Moses Dickson, James Milton Turner, and other local African American leaders took action. They wanted to help their fellow black citizens. They also wanted to keep whites from thinking that all blacks were poor and unequal to them.

A new group called the Committee of Twenty-Five gave the migrants places to stay and help getting where they wanted to go (although some chose to stay in St. Louis). Another group, the Colored Immigration Aid Society, raised money to support new black colonies in the West. Between 1916 and 1970, even more African Americans left the South. More than 6 million men, women, and children fled to the North, Midwest, and West. Most wound up in big cities such as New York, Chicago, St. Louis, and Los Angeles. This movement of black people is known as the Great Migration.

For Southern blacks who settled in the Midwest and North, life was better in some ways. They could usually find work, and their children could get a better education. But they were still unequal to white people. Inequality and injustice touched every part of daily life, from school and housing to work and entertainment.

MOSES DICKSON (1824–1901)

Moses Dickson spent his early life trying to get rid of slavery. In 1846 he co-founded a secret group, the Knights of Liberty. Dickson and the Knights were going to use weapons to fight back against slavery and set slaves free.

When Dickson saw that the Civil War was coming, he and the Knights changed plans. They helped enslaved people get away on the Underground Railroad, which wasn't a railroad at all. It was really a network of safe houses and people who helped slaves run away to the North.

During the Civil War, Dickson fought in the Northern army. After the war he became a minister. Dickson also did other things:

HERE AND NOW

- He started the Knights and Daughters of Tabor, a self-help group for African Americans.
- He worked with Charlton Tandy on the Colored Refugee Relief Board to help Southern blacks in St. Louis.
- He co-founded Lincoln Institute (now Lincoln University) in Jefferson City.

Father Dickson Cemetery in Crestwood is named for him.

Having greater access to more civil rights made African Americans who moved north feel safer and happier. What are ways your community makes all people feel safe and happy?

CHAPTER 7
FIGHTING FOR EQUAL SCHOOLS

When Missouri first became a state, both blacks and whites could go to school. Sometimes they even studied together. That changed in 1847 when the state said blacks couldn't go to school. Anyone who taught them how to read or write would have to pay money, spend time in jail, or both.

Some churches found a way around the law. They said they were just teaching about God and faith at Sunday school. Some people taught "sewing classes" where black students pretended to be learning to sew but were really learning how to read and write.

John Berry Meachum, a black minister, tried to get around the law too. He ran a school in the basement of his First Baptist Church, but the police shut it down. He didn't give up though! Stories handed down through families say he bought a steamboat and reopened his school on the Mississippi River. Because the river wasn't part of Missouri, he could teach without the police stopping him.

When the Civil War ended in 1865, Missouri promised free public school to everyone between the ages of 5 and 21. This new law allowed separate schools for blacks. It also said that state money should be given out based on how many students were in a school, not skin color. James Milton Turner and other state education leaders went around Missouri making sure schools followed the law. Yet public schools still weren't equal in St. Louis. Sumner High School is a good example of this.

JAMES MILTON TURNER (1840–1915)

James Milton Turner was born into slavery. He was freed at age 4 after his father bought his freedom. Turner went to secret schools on both sides of the river. He even started college at age 14.

After the Civil War, Turner helped raise money to start Lincoln Institute, a black college in Jefferson City. He made sure the school became a training place for black teachers. Today the school is called Lincoln University, and students of all races go there.

Turner also led the Missouri Equal Rights League. This group fought to get voting rights for black men. In 1871 he became the U.S. ambassador to the African country of Liberia. This made him the second black U.S. diplomat.

He returned to St. Louis eight years later and helped free Native Americans who'd been slaves in the Indian territories. He died in 1915 and is buried at Father Dickson Cemetery.

THE MEACHUMS

John Berry Meachum was an impressive person. While enslaved, he saved up enough money to buy freedom for himself; his parents; his siblings; his kids; and his wife, Mary.

Once free, he moved to St. Louis. He earned money by doing carpentry and making cabinets. He bought more than 20 slaves, trained them, and let them earn their freedom. Later on he became a minister and started the First Baptist Church. It's the oldest black church in St. Louis.

Both Meachums also helped with the Underground Railroad. Mary kept helping enslaved people cross over to Illinois after John died in 1854. She was arrested for this the next year. Today the Mary Meachum Freedom Crossing, on the Riverfront Trail about three miles north of the Arch, marks the spot where nine slaves aided by Mary tried to cross the river.

John Berry Meachum is buried at Bellefontaine Cemetery. Mary's final resting place is unknown.

Sumner opened in 1875 and was the first black high school west of the Mississippi River. Yet the principal and teachers were white. Three existing black grade schools also shared the building, which was rundown and in a noisy part of downtown. From it you could see the place where criminals who'd been sentenced to death were killed and the building where the city put dead bodies. So even though state law said black and white schools had to be equal, St. Louis had given blacks a lesser school.

By the early 1900s, the Sumner building was in even worse shape. The students weren't much better off. They were learning skills that would get them low-paying jobs, like how to fix things, cook, and sew, while students at white schools learned skills that would get them better-paying jobs, like grammar and spelling. Sumner lacked in other ways too. It didn't have a gym, proper restrooms, an auditorium, a library, or clubs like debate or orchestra—all things taken for granted in the city's white high schools.

A group called the Colored Citizens' Council (CCC), led by Rev. George Stevens, came together to push for a new Sumner High School. In 1907 the CCC put out a 12-page booklet that showed how most African Americans had moved away from downtown. Many had gone to a new area northwest of downtown called the Ville. The CCC argued that Sumner families wanted their high school to be where they were. The St. Louis Board of Education agreed to build a new Sumner in the Ville—for much less money than it had spent on a recent white school building.

The new Sumner opened in 1910. This time the principal, Frank Williams, was African American. He turned the school into a place where students learned math, reading, writing, history, and more, just like students did at white high schools. He also helped start a teacher-training program at Sumner to make sure there would be more African American teachers who could teach at black schools.

One of these teachers was Dr. Herman Dreer. While at Sumner, he realized black students didn't know much about their past. He made a plan to change this by getting African American history into black classrooms. First he brought Negro History Week to St. Louis in February 1927. Then he spent Saturdays training other teachers on how to teach African American history. Thanks to Dreer, St. Louis celebrated black history in February for nearly 50 years before the U.S. government made it Black History Month.

Sumner High School moved to 4248 Cottage Avenue in 1910 and is still there today.

REV. GEORGE STEVENS (1861–1941)

George Stevens was a very well-educated minister. He came to St. Louis's Central Baptist Church in 1903 from churches in New York and Boston. During a 1905 program at the church, he said, "The time for black men to claim and expect every right and consideration, which every other man claims and should expect, is now."

He strongly believed that schools should be equal. He thought keeping blacks in one school and whites in another made people less trusting. Stevens fought hard for equal housing in St. Louis too.

Rev. George Stevens, ca. 1927. From *History of Central Baptist Church*, Missouri Historical Society.

Between Sumner's founding and its move, the U.S. Supreme Court ruled on a case called *Plessy v. Ferguson*. "Separate but equal" was now okay. This meant states could keep blacks and whites apart by law in schools, restaurants, bathrooms, and more. The black option just had to be equal to the white one. But separate was never truly equal. White people were always taken care of first. Black people got what was left.

The NAACP (National Association for the Advancement of Colored People) fought back. Its lawyers filed lawsuits against the "equal" promise of "separate but equal." The NAACP figured that school and state leaders wouldn't want to spend the money to build truly equal schools for African Americans and that they'd just let black students into the white schools instead. The group's efforts got national attention with the second important civil rights lawsuit from St. Louis to make it to the Supreme Court: *Gaines v. Canada*.

ST. LOUIS, CIVIL RIGHTS, AND THE U.S. SUPREME COURT: *GAINES V. CANADA*

THE PEOPLE

- Lloyd Gaines, a student trying to enter the University of Missouri Law School
- Cy Woodson Canada, the school's registrar

THE BACKGROUND

Lloyd Gaines was a star student. He was valedictorian at Vashon High School, and he did well in college too. After graduating from Lincoln University, he wanted to go to law school at the University of Missouri. The school didn't want to let him in because he was black.

The State of Missouri said it would pay for Gaines to study law somewhere else. Gaines and his NAACP lawyers—Sidney Redmond, Henry Espy, Charles Hamilton Houston, and Thurgood Marshall—turned down the offer. They argued that Gaines would need to know Missouri law and have local contacts to be a good lawyer. Because the University of Missouri Law School was the only law school in the state, there was no "separate but equal" place he could go. Missouri either had to let Gaines into the school or provide a separate, equal law school for black students.

Gaines and his lawyers lost in both the county and state courts. These courts said the offer to pay for an out-of-state law school was good enough. They also said that keeping white and black students apart was best for both groups. Next, Gaines and his lawyers asked the U.S. Supreme Court to review their appeal.

THE CASE

In November 1938 lawyers for both sides appeared before the Supreme Court. Gaines's team said it was unfair to keep him out of Missouri's law school when there was no equal, separate school he could go to instead. His lawyers again turned down the offer of money for an out-of-state law school.

Lloyd Gaines, 1931. From the Collections of the St. Louis Mercantile Library at the University of Missouri–St. Louis.

THE DECISION

In a 6–2 vote, the Supreme Court decided that because Missouri made local law school an option for one group, it had to make local law school open to all groups. The school either had to let Gaines in or create an equal option within the state.

THE AFTERMATH

The State of Missouri chose to set up a "separate but equal" law school for African Americans. It turned the old Poro College building in the Ville neighborhood into the new Lincoln University School of Law. Black lawyers studied there for almost 20 years until it became part of the University of Missouri Law School.

Gaines didn't go to the school though. He disappeared after the Supreme Court case. No one knows what happened to him.

THE LEGACY

The *Gaines* case was a huge step toward overturning the "separate but equal" ruling from *Plessy v. Ferguson*. Sixteen years later, in 1954, the Supreme Court heard a case called *Brown v. Board of Education of Topeka, Kansas*. In it the Court ruled that keeping black and white students apart in public schools was illegal. Separate no longer meant equal in the eyes of the law.

HERE AND NOW

Lincoln University School of Law once stood here. Its building was torn down in the late 1960s and replaced by the James House apartments.

The *Gaines* case inspired others to sue for admission to schools. Lucile Bluford made it into the University of Missouri's graduate program for journalism—until the school found out she was black. She filed a lawsuit and applied 11 more times, but the school wouldn't let her back in. When the Missouri Supreme Court said the University of Missouri had to admit her, the journalism school closed its graduate program. It said too many of its professors and students were fighting in World War II for it to stay open. The University of Missouri didn't let in its first African American students until 1950.

In 1944, Saint Louis University, a private Catholic school, became the first all-white university in Missouri to accept African American students. Two years later, Archbishop Joseph Ritter opened all of St. Louis's Catholic grade schools and high schools to black students. Angry white parents protested, but the archbishop didn't back down.

After pressure from NAACP lawyers and a student group, Washington University in St. Louis also let black students in. The medical and social work programs started taking African Americans in 1947. By the fall of 1952, all of the school was opened to blacks.

How do you think the right to go to school and get an education affects other civil rights?

CHAPTER 8
FIGHTING FOR EQUAL HOUSING

As slavery faded away, more African Americans could make and keep money for their work. They wanted to use that money to rent or buy their own places to live. This concerned many white people who wanted to keep African Americans out of their neighborhoods.

Starting in 1915, several white neighborhoods came together. Their goal? To get voters to say yes to a new law that said a person couldn't buy a home on a block where more than 75 percent of people living there were a different race. So a black family couldn't move to a mostly white block. A white family couldn't move to a mostly black block either.

African Americans spoke out against the proposed law. Rev. George Stevens even wrote a powerful pamphlet titled *Negro Segregation: A Measure to Assassinate a Race in St. Louis, Missouri*. But blacks weren't alone. The *St. Louis Post-Dispatch* (a white newspaper), the local Jewish community, and most of the city's lawmakers spoke out too.

A Shaming Stigma Upon St. Louis
would be Race Segregation By Law

This picture presents one of a number of objectionable results that would follow the adoption of the proposed ordinances

(THE GREAT DIVIDE—Fitzpatrick in St. Louis Post-Dispatch, Feb. 18)

A Segregation Law would be an Illegal Wrong to the Negro Race. It would be a lasting *Shame and Disgrace* to the White Race, which inflicted such a wrong.

Scratch YES! February 29. Vote NO!!

This editorial cartoon by Daniel Fitzpatrick appeared in the *Post-Dispatch* in February 1916. Missouri Historical Society.

VIEWS & NEWS

People wrote several letters to the editor of the *St. Louis Post-Dispatch* about the proposed law. Some supported it; others condemned it.

A Discouraged Home Owner, Jan. 22, 1916: When I was young, my husband built a nice home on Clark avenue. The negro invaded, ruined the value of my home, and made it impossible for us to invite friends to visit us.

The Cost of Progress, Feb. 29, 1916: Ordinances must be reasonable. A law which restricts the equal rights of citizens--impairs the use and value of one man's property in order that another may be free from annoyance, does not commend itself to the impartial mind.

HOMER G. PHILLIPS (1880–1931)

Homer G. Phillips was a lawyer for the NAACP. He worked on many cases. One of these was the NAACP's fight against the 1916 housing law. He also helped victims of the 1917 race riot in East St. Louis.

Phillips noticed that black patients and doctors weren't treated equally in local hospitals, so he worked to change this. He became the driving force behind the creation of a hospital for African Americans. It opened in the Ville neighborhood in 1937 and was named for him. Many black doctors trained and worked there until it closed in the late 1970s.

The local NAACP (National Association for the Advancement of Colored People) also fought the housing law. The branch had formed in 1914 and was made up of white and black members. It worked very hard to get people to vote no on the law in the spring 1916 election. Two NAACP lawyers, Homer G. Phillips and George Vaughn, also spent hours preparing court cases to challenge the law.

In the end, the law passed by a huge amount. It didn't last for long, though. The next year, the U.S. Supreme Court ruled that a similar Kentucky law was illegal, which made the St. Louis law illegal too.

Without a law on their side, many St. Louis whites next tried a different approach. Realtors, people who help others buy and sell homes, wouldn't show black buyers homes in white neighborhoods. Some white homeowners also made promises with other white homeowners nearby. They vowed not to sell their houses to people who weren't white.

One day in 1945 the black Shelley family bought a house in a place where the homeowners had made such a promise to each other. Out of this came the third major St. Louis civil rights lawsuit to end up in the U.S. Supreme Court.

ST. LOUIS, CIVIL RIGHTS, AND THE U.S. SUPREME COURT: *SHELLEY V. KRAEMER*

THE PEOPLE

- J. D. and Ethel Shelley, owners of 4600 Labadie Avenue
- Fern and Louis Kraemer, the Shelleys' neighbors

THE BACKGROUND

In 1945, African Americans J. D. and Ethel Shelley proudly bought a house at 4600 Labadie Avenue. At last they had a place big enough for them and their six children. They didn't know that in 1911 people in the neighborhood had signed a *restrictive covenant*. This document said only white people could buy houses in the neighborhood for the next 50 years.

After the Shelleys moved in, a neighborhood group got Fern and Louis Kraemer to file a lawsuit against the family. It said the Shelleys broke the law by being black and buying a home in the white neighborhood.

The first court sided with the Shelleys. Then the Missouri Supreme Court sided with the Kraemers. George Vaughn, the Shelleys' lawyer, appealed to the U.S. Supreme Court in 1947.

The Shelley family in their home at 4600 Labadie Ave. Courtesy of the Copeland Collection.

THE CASE

Vaughn stood before the Court and gave these reasons for why the Shelleys should win:

- Not every homeowner on the block had signed the 1911 agreement.
- A few black families had lived on the block for years.
- Denying blacks the same rights as whites to buy and sell property went against the 14th Amendment, which gives all U.S. citizens the same rights.

The U.S. government also supported the Shelleys. It filed its first-ever civil rights "friend of the court" document on their behalf.

THE DECISION

A plaque in front of 4600 Labadie Ave. today describes the importance of the Shelleys' home.

The Supreme Court ruled in favor of the Shelleys. Restrictive covenants were no longer legal.

THE AFTERMATH

The Shelleys lived at 4600 Labadie Avenue until June 1961. The house became a National Historic Landmark in 1990.

THE LEGACY

Shelley v. Kraemer helped chip away at the idea of "separate but equal" treatment of blacks and whites. As J. D. Shelley put it years later: "The way I see it, it was a good thing that we done this case. When all this happened, when I bought the property, I didn't think there was going to be anything about it. But I knowed it was important. We was the first ones to live where they said colored can't live."

48

GEORGE VAUGHN (1882–1950)

George Vaughn, the son of former slaves, was a well-known NAACP lawyer. His most famous case? His 1948 victory in the U.S. Supreme Court on behalf of J. D. and Ethel Shelley. Vaughn died two years later.

Despite winning the *Shelley* case, local African Americans still had to fight for equal housing into the 1950s. This time they were pushing back against the city and federal governments.

A city agency called the St. Louis Housing Authority was in charge of four *housing projects*. These were big buildings full of apartments for people who couldn't afford to live anywhere else. The City of St. Louis paid for them. Two of the buildings were just for black families. The other two were just for white families.

One of the white housing projects was opened in 1953. Two years later, black families were still waiting for theirs. Attorney Frankie Muse Freeman took the St. Louis Housing Authority to court to get the "color line" in public housing removed. She won! A federal judge ordered all public housing projects in St. Louis be open to people of all races.

One final, major step toward equal housing came out of St. Louis in the 1960s. Joseph and Barbara Jones were looking to buy a house. The Paddock Woods subdivision caught their eye, so they asked the builder about buying a home there. They were told they couldn't buy one because Joseph was African American. The fourth major St. Louis civil rights case to make it to the U.S. Supreme Court soon followed.

What do you think it means that the path to full civil rights for African Americans has often been "one step forward, two steps back, take a detour, get back on track"?

FRANKIE MUSE FREEMAN (b. 1916)

Frankie Muse Freeman is a St. Louis legend. After graduating from law school, she couldn't get a job in St. Louis's mostly white, mostly male law firms. But that didn't stop her! She started her own firm and worked on many NAACP cases alongside the group's star male lawyers.

In 1964, President Lyndon Johnson made Freeman the first woman to serve on the U.S. Commission on Civil Rights. Part of this group's work was to study how black and white students were kept apart in public schools. Freeman told the president that black and white students "would be less likely to make [later] decisions based on race or class if they get to know one another. The cycle must be broken in classrooms."

Frankie Muse Freeman in her law office, ca. 1978. Missouri Historical Society.

She has been a judge and a board member of many local groups.

ST. LOUIS, CIVIL RIGHTS, AND THE U.S. SUPREME COURT: *JONES V. ALFRED H. MAYER CO.*

THE PEOPLE

- Joseph and Barbara Jones, would-be homeowners in Paddock Woods
- Alfred H. Mayer, housing and subdivision builder with his own company

THE BACKGROUND

In 1960s St. Louis, new neighborhoods called subdivisions were split by race. Some were known to be "for whites" or "for blacks" only. Others had rules about not selling to black buyers in "white" neighborhoods. That's the message Joseph and Barbara Jones were given when they tried to buy a house in the Paddock Woods subdivision.

A local housing rights group paired the Joneses with lawyer Samuel Liberman II. He said that the Civil Rights Act of 1866 gave blacks and whites equal rights to property ownership.

The lower court and state appeals court disagreed. They ruled that the 1866 law was meant to say what the government could do, not what a private seller could do. The Joneses appealed to the U.S. Supreme Court in 1968.

Joseph and Barbara Jones. Photo by Buel White. Courtesy of *St. Louis Post-Dispatch*.

THE CASE

Mayer's company claimed that it could do whatever it wanted because it was a private business. But the national feelings were changing on this and other questions of civil rights.

Right when the Court was hearing the *Jones* case, Dr. Martin Luther King Jr. was killed in Memphis, Tennessee. Fear and sadness about how blacks and whites interacted prompted the U.S. Congress to quickly pass the Fair Housing Act of 1968. This law said that race couldn't play a part in buying or selling a home.

THE DECISION

In a 7–2 decision, the Supreme Court ruled that the 1866 Civil Rights Act applied to both private sellers and the government. No person, business, or government could deny someone a home based on race.

THE AFTERMATH

The Joneses never got to live in Paddock Woods. By the time they won their case, all the houses there had been sold.

As for Mayer, it turns out he actually gave money to help pay for the Joneses' first lawsuit. He was a business owner and likely wanted to be able to sell to any buyer, white or black.

THE LEGACY

The *Jones* case was a solid win in the fight for equal housing. But the fact that it cites so much of the 1866 law shows how the path toward full civil rights for African Americans has often been a "one step forward, two steps back, take a detour, get back on track" route. Advocates had to return to courts again and again just to ensure basic rights and equal freedoms.

CHAPTER 9
FIGHTING FOR EQUAL WORK

When big cities like St. Louis, Detroit, and Pittsburgh began booming, lots of jobs followed. Many African Americans from rural areas or the South moved closer to these cities in search of work.

By the 1910s, East St. Louis, located just across the Mississippi River in Illinois, was home to many businesses with many jobs. About 10,000 black people had come to the area hoping to get one of them.

The white workers already in East St. Louis worried about losing their jobs to black workers. They also feared having to take pay cuts if African Americans would work for less money than they would.

Rich factory owners did nothing to help calm these fears. It was good for them if they had to pay people less. Sometimes they even added to the problems by luring more black workers to town with promises of jobs.

Things came to a head in the summer of 1917. Workers were strik- ing at some factories. White people were hurting black people. False rumors about black acts against whites were spreading. The city was on edge.

It exploded on July 2, 1917, in one of the longest and deadliest race riots of the time. Large groups of white people set fire to black homes and apartment buildings. The people inside had to choose between being burned or running outside where they might be shot by men with guns.

Between 40 and 200 African Americans were killed in the riot. Some 600 others were left homeless. Many of them fled across the river.

St. Louis's leaders opened shelters and feeding centers. NAACP lawyers gave free help to people who wanted to sue for the loss of their homes and so much more. A local chapter of the Urban League also formed to help the East St. Louis refugees.

A fire near the East St. Louis Public Library during the 1917 race riot.
Missouri Historical Society.

World War I ended the next year. Many African American soldiers had fought in it. They had been willing to risk their lives for their country, but their country still didn't grant them equal rights back home. For many, this was a turning point. They began to demand their rights.

One way they did this was through the Don't Buy Where You Can't Work campaign. This was a national push to get black people to spend their money only in places that had black workers. The goal was to convince businesses in African American areas to hire black workers if they didn't have any. Judge Nathan B. Young brought the campaign to St. Louis. It helped get black employees hired at dairies, bakeries, and other stores.

JUDGE NATHAN B. YOUNG (1894–1993)

Nathan B. Young was a lawyer and judge who helped co-found *The St. Louis American*. This African American newspaper is still published today. Young ran the paper's editorial page for 42 years. There he shared his thoughts on jobs, schools, area politics, and local civil rights struggles.

A 1964 piece he wrote for the paper declared St. Louis the "Number One City in Civil Rights History" based on the number of landmark U.S. Supreme Court civil rights cases that started here.

The Colored Clerks' Circle was another St. Louis arm of the Don't Buy Where You Can't Work campaign. This group of black men and women held signs and walked in front of stores in black neighborhoods that only hired blacks as janitors. They demanded better jobs for African Americans.

Lawyer David Grant was a driving force behind the Colored Clerks' Circle. He went on to become a leader in the March on Washington Movement (MOWM), which started in 1941. MOWM happened all over the United States but was very strong in St. Louis. It had three goals:

- to help African Americans get government and military jobs
- to get blacks working in factories that made products for the war effort
- to show how a large group of black citizens could force change without violence

MOWM was going to hold a march in Washington, DC, in the summer of 1941 to make its point. Before the march could happen, though, President Franklin D. Roosevelt told military factories to hire black people. This was enough to stop the march, but MOWM's ideas lived on.

Organizers began to hold rallies in cities around the country. The August 1942 MOWM meeting in St. Louis was one of the biggest. David Grant, T. D. McNeal, and other leaders spoke about peaceful protesting and marching as ways to create change.

What do you think it means for a protest to be "peaceful"? What are some examples of peaceful protests? What are some benefits to using peaceful protests?

DAVID GRANT (1903–1985)

David Grant was a leading activist in St. Louis. He helped start the city's first protest for equal jobs for black workers. He also led protests at Carter Carburetor, Jefferson Bank, and Southwestern Bell.

Grant was a top lawyer too. He led the 1945 case to get Washington University in St. Louis to accept black students. He was also an active Democrat at a time when most African Americans were Republicans.

Grant's south St. Louis home was a safe space for black artists, musicians, writers, and thinkers who came to the area.

David Grant, 1937. Courtesy of Gail Milissa Grant.

MOWM's first target for equal treatment was Carter Carburetor. This factory made parts for military vehicles during World War II, but it didn't have any black workers. More than 400 people marched from nearby Tandy Park to the factory at Grand Boulevard and St. Louis Avenue in late summer 1942. The march made national headlines in African American newspapers, but the factory never did hire any black workers.

MOWM had better luck the next year. After the Southwestern Bell phone company refused to hire black phone operators, MOWM held protests outside the company's downtown headquarters. But that's not all! MOWM also had more than 200 black customers pay their September phone bills entirely with pennies. After that, the phone company agreed to hire African Americans and open an office in a black neighborhood.

Yet by 1963 some businesses still hadn't hired African Americans for jobs that needed special training. One of these businesses was the Jefferson Bank and Trust Company. It hired black workers but wouldn't let them handle the money.

The St. Louis chapter of CORE (Committee of Racial Equality) held a sit-in at the bank. On August 30, 1963, people came to the lobby, sat down, and started singing. They also walked outside the building and carried signs. The protest was largely peaceful, yet many people were arrested. Some also were given large fines and had to spend time in jail. City alderman William L. Clay Sr. was one of those arrested for taking part in the protest.

Percy Green and other new, young leaders filled in for the jailed protesters. They kept the pressure on Jefferson Bank. Finally, on March 31, 1964, the bank agreed to hire six black tellers.

City alderman William L. Clay Sr. (center, seated) among fellow Jefferson Bank protesters. Courtesy of *The St. Louis American*.

Jefferson Bank wasn't any worse than most other white-owned businesses in St. Louis. But by saying for so long that it wouldn't hire blacks for any jobs but the very lowest ones, it had made itself an easy target.

The Jefferson Bank protests were a turning point in St. Louis civil rights history for four big reasons:

- Large groups of ordinary people showed up day after day.
- A new, young set of leaders emerged.
- Police arrested large groups of people in response to protests—a first in St. Louis.
- The protesters showed long-term commitment.

VIEWS & NEWS

Here's what activist Margaret Bush Wilson had to say about the Jefferson Bank protests during a 1998 interview with Nine Network of Public Media:

> Well, Jefferson Bank, as you know, was a protest about jobs and the banks. It focused on one bank, primarily because that bank had been sitting in the black community and had moved to the edge of it. And when they were in the black community, they had had a couple of black employees, but when they moved to their brand-new, beautiful site—[pshht]. And that was terrible, really. And it was an initiative of the Committee on Racial Equality, CORE. At the time, I was state president of NAACP. So it was CORE's initiative, and they were in the midst of having discussions with this bank. And the discussions broke down, and they decided they'd just go sit in. And I guess the phrase is "it got out of hand." [laughter]
>
> It was a defining moment for this city, though, in retrospect, because 'til then there had been no black people working in any bank above the menial level. Now, if you wander around, you will see our people everywhere. You know, it's a given. In fact, I walked into one of the branches of the Mercantile Bank recently, and I looked around and everyone in the room, behind the counter, was African American. I just chuckled because back in those days there were none.

PERCY GREEN (b. 1935)

Percy Green is a St. Louis–born activist. He took part in the 1963 Jefferson Bank protest. After this, Green left CORE and started ACTION (Action Council to Improve Opportunities for Negroes). This group was a homegrown answer to St. Louis's racial problems. Because no larger, national group was in charge of ACTION, the group could take "action" as it saw fit. One way was with "stick-ins," where ACTION members poured syrup on businesses' door handles and floors to protest what they saw as unjust treatment.

Green is also known for climbing up the side of the Gateway Arch as it was being built. He and Richard Daly, a white student, made the climb to protest the lack of black people on the project.

Green is still active in local politics and civil rights causes.

Percy Green, ca. 1970. Missouri Historical Society.

CHAPTER 10
FIGHTING FOR EQUAL ENTERTAINMENT

Going to a movie. Swimming at a public pool. Grabbing a bite to eat with friends. These basic entertainments are the same for blacks and whites in St. Louis now, but they weren't always.

At movie and theatre performances, black people had to sit high up in the balcony. Sometimes they were only allowed to be there on certain days. But African Americans didn't settle for this treatment. One man, Henry Winfield Wheeler, made protesting at such theaters into a lifelong volunteer project.

This chapter tells us about activists who stood up for their rights to go to restaurants, movie theaters, pools, and other fun places. Where is a place that you really like to go? What would you do if someone tried to stop you from going there?

HENRY WINFIELD WHEELER (1888–1964)

Henry Winfield Wheeler was known as Mr. Civil Rights here in St. Louis. While working at the post office, he fought against lunchrooms that kept blacks and whites apart. He also spoke out about how the better post office jobs went to white workers, not blacks.

He was a founding member of the local NAACP branch. He also protested with the Colored Clerks' Circle and joined the March on Washington Movement. He was even elected twice to the Missouri House of Representatives.

Despite all of this, Wheeler may be best known for the seven years he spent protesting in

Henry Winfield Wheeler. From the Collections of the St. Louis Mercantile Library at the University of Missouri–St. Louis.

front of the American Theatre, which limited black people to the balcony. In October 1952 the American made all of its seats open to everyone. Wheeler had finally won!

Most of the fight for equal entertainment was peaceful. The 1949 riot at Fairground Park was different. That summer, St. Louis had opened its pools to all swimmers. (Before this, black children and white children swam in separate pools.)

On June 21 of that year, a group of African American kids showed up at the Fairground Park Pool ready to swim. Hundreds of angry white people met them. Many carried baseball bats, sticks, and clubs. They wanted to hurt the black swimmers and scare them off. It took 12 hours and

A white teen taunting black boys outside of the Fairground Park Pool, June 1949. From the Collections of the St. Louis Mercantile Library at the University of Missouri–St. Louis.

hundreds of police officers to calm everyone down. Dozens of people got hurt, and police had to clear away about 5,000 people.

In response, St. Louis's mayor made the city's swimming pools separate again. African Americans pushed back. They showed up at Fairground Park Pool and demanded to be let in. Some came alone. Others came with lawyers. In July 1950 a judge ordered the city's pools to be opened to all races once more.

Lunch counters and restaurants also tried to limit where African Americans could be. They didn't count on people pushing back. In 1944 groups of black and white women went to the lunch counters at three downtown St. Louis department stores. They sat down and didn't leave until they were served. These sit-ins were some of the first ones in the country.

By the late 1940s, CORE (Committee of Racial Equality) had joined the push for equal treatment at lunch counters and restaurants. Groups of black and white men and women sat in at the Stix, Baer & Fuller department store for 18 months. They were there so often that Stix customers began asking about the protests. This gave CORE members a chance to explain and get more people on their side. Still, the Stix owners refused to serve blacks and whites equally. CORE eventually focused on other sites and tactics.

Finally, in June 1961, St. Louis passed a law about public places. It said that public business that offered food, shelter, entertainment, play, safety, or health had to treat blacks and whites equally. (Private clubs still didn't have to let black people in.)

THE YOUNGEST CIVIL RIGHTS LEADERS

From the 1940s through the 1960s, more and more young people joined civil rights groups in St. Louis. Many saw themselves as the next generation of civil rights leaders. Norman Seay, who co-founded CORE while still in high school, expressed it well:

Norman Seay (right) at a 1969 ACTION rally. Missouri Historical Society.

"I tell people all the time we were before the civil rights movement started because the civil rights movement started, the one we know about, was Martin Luther King and Rosa Parks in 1955. We were 1947 and we were creating havoc. Here this integrated group of youngsters knocking on doors, talking . . . about integration, about employing African Americans, about upgrading them . . . we were change agents."

Seay and others, including Maggie and Irv Dagen, Billie Teneau, and Charles and Marian Oldham, made St. Louis's CORE chapter a strong one. They touched every major civil rights issue of their time. They even had a great effect on CORE's success nationwide.

The NAACP Youth Council also played a big role in St. Louis's civil rights story. Bill Clay revived the chapter in 1955 after returning home from serving in the U.S. Army. Clay and other Youth Council members protested at lunch counters and restaurants that hired whites only and kept blacks and whites apart to eat. Their protests upset the older NAACP members, who saw the youth as impatient and out of line. The Youth Council soon lost its charter and had to stop protesting.

Margaret Bush Wilson. Missouri Historical Society.

In the late 1950s, two women helped bring the Youth Council back to life. Margaret Bush Wilson was the first female president of St. Louis's NAACP. Fredda Witherspoon was a lifetime NAACP member. They knew that young people would demand change in a short timeframe. Wilson and Witherspoon got many students from Vashon High School—as well as other high schools and colleges—to join the new Youth Council. These students protested outside department stores and diners, leading to changes at some.

CHAPTER II

WHAT'S NEXT?

The fight for civil rights didn't end in the 1960s or 1970s. A powerful example of that fact happened in recent memory in Ferguson, Missouri.

On August 9, 2014, Michael Brown, an African American teen, was shot and killed by a white police officer. Many stories were told about how and why the shooting happened. These stories don't all agree on the facts. What people do agree on is that Brown didn't have a gun or knife with him when he was killed.

Shortly after the shooting, large crowds of people came to the spot where Brown died. Many were upset that his body had been left on the street for hours. Others were angry about how the police treated black people. Some spoke out against the violence in their neighborhoods. Others demanded better access to jobs and schools for African Americans. Still others protested that courts and judges didn't treat blacks and whites equally when giving punishments.

People protested for weeks. There were nights when some people in the crowd threw things and started fires. There were nights when the police drove armed tanks through the streets and wore special riot gear to face protesters. Emotional photos were splashed across newspaper pages and the Internet. The world was watching.

Was Ferguson the start of a new civil rights movement? Or will it become an overlooked moment? The answer remains to be seen.

✎ *African Americans are still fighting for equal civil rights. What lessons can we take from past St. Louis civil rights leaders to make sure everyone is treated fairly today?*

VIEWS & NEWS

Angela "Miss Angie the DJ" Whitman, a protest leader, sat down with the Missouri History Museum in 2015 to discuss the day Michael Brown was shot and killed:

> It was so many people that were crying; it was a lot of cussing going on. It was a lot of people just . . . everybody showed their feelings, their emotions, whether it was angry, whether it was in tears, whether they would kneel down, whether they were embracing one another. It was that bad. And I love God, so for me I have to keep praying. You know, God say, "Don't cease from praying, continue to pray." And I had seen so many people that I knew, and it was like, you just . . . I think it had came to a point in those hours after he had died where people were just lost, like, nobody knew what to do with the anger. Nobody knew what to do with what they feel. And it was . . . it was bad.

CHAPTER 12
WHAT CAN YOU DO?

We've come a long way, but even today people are often still treated differently because of their skin color. So what can you do to help change that?

Learn everything you can. Read about the history of civil rights in our city and state. Talk to adults you respect about what life was like when they were growing up.

Speak out about what you learn. If you see people aren't being treated fairly, point it out.

When you hear local schools, jobs, voting, crime, and housing being discussed, ask smart questions about what's happening and why. Then demand real answers.

Find local groups and programs that support equal rights. Many schools, clubs, and faith communities offer these. If you have younger brothers or sisters, sign up your family for We Stories, a reading program that uses storybooks to help families talk about race.

Most important, remember that anyone can be an activist. You just have to be willing to stand up for what you believe is right.

In 1964, Judge Nathan B. Young declared St. Louis the Number One City in Civil Rights History. Before reading this book, how would you have responded to Judge Young's claim? How would you respond now? Do you agree? Why or why not?

RECOMMENDED READING

A Dream of Freedom: The Civil Rights Movement from 1954 to 1968 by Diane McWhorter (Scholastic, 2004).

Freedom's Children: Young Civil Rights Activists Tell Their Own Stories by Ellen S. Levine (Puffin Books, 2014).

Marching for Freedom: Walk Together, Children, and Don't You Grow Weary by Elizabeth Partridge (Viking Books, 2009).

Remember: The Journey to School Integration by Toni Morrison (Houghton Mifflin, 2004).

Rosa Parks: My Story by Rosa Parks and James Haskins (Distributed by Paw Prints/Baker & Taylor, 2009).

Sit-In: How Four Friends Stood Up by Sitting Down by Andrea Davis Pinkney (Little, Brown, 2010).

We Shall Overcome: A Song That Changed the World by Stuart Stotts and Terrance Cummings (Clarion Books, 2010).

What Was the March on Washington? by Kathleen Krull and Tim Tomkinson (Scholastic, 2016).

INDEX

Bluford, Lucile, 41
Brown, Michael, 71

Clay, William L., Sr., 60, 61, 69

Dagen, Irv and Maggie, 68
Dickson, Moses, 27, 28–29
Dreer, Dr. Herman, 35

Freeman, Frankie Muse, 50–51

Gaines, Lloyd, 38–41
Grant, David, 58, 59
Green, Percy, 60, 63

Jones, Joseph and Barbara, 50, 52–54

Keckley, Elizabeth "Lizzie," 7

Lovejoy, Elijah P., 13

McNeal, T. D., 58
Meachum, John Berry and Mary,
    30, 32–33

Oldham, Charles and Marian, 68

Phillips, Homer G., 44, 45

Redmond, Sidney, 38

Scott, Dred and Harriet, 15–18
Seay, Norman, 68
Shelley, Ethel and J. D., 46–48
Stevens, Rev. George, 34, 36, 42

Tandy, Charlton, 23, 24–25, 27, 28
Teneau, Billie, 68
Turner, James Milton, 27, 30, 31

Vaughn, George, 45, 46–47, 49

Wheeler, Henry Winfield, 64, 65
Whitman, Angela "Miss Angie the DJ," 72
Wilson, Margaret Bush, 62, 69
Winny, 14
Witherspoon, Fredda, 69

Young, Judge Nathan B., 3, 56, 57

© 2017 by the Missouri History Museum Press
ISBN 978-1-883982-91-1

Library of Congress Cataloging-in-Publication Data
Names: Doyle, Amanda E., author. | Adams, Melanie A, 1969- author.
Title: Standing up for civil rights in St. Louis / by Amanda E. Doyle and Melanie A. Adams.
Description: St. Louis : Missouri History Museum Press, Distributed by University of Chicago Press, [2017] | Includes bibliographical references and index. | Audience: Grades 4-6.
Identifiers: LCCN 2017028679 | ISBN 9781883982911 (pbk. : alk. paper)
Subjects: LCSH: African Americans--Civil rights--Missouri--Saint Louis--Juvenile literature. | Civil rights movements--Missouri--Saint Louis--History--Juvenile literature. | African Americans--Civil rights--History--Juvenile literature. | Civil rights movements--United States--History--Juvenile literature.
Classification: LCC F474.S29 D69 2017 | DDC 323.1196/073077866--dc23
LC record available at https://lccn.loc.gov/2017028679

Cover design: Wade Howell
Illustrations: Darnell Chambers
Contemporary photos: Cary Horton
Doyle photo: David Lancaster
Adams photo: Brady Willette

Printed and bound in the United States by Sheridan Books, Inc.
Distributed by University of Chicago Press